GEMINI

HOROSCOPE

& ASTROLOGY

2021

Published by Mystic Cat Press

Suite SM-2380-6403

14601 North Bybee Lake Court

Portland, Oregon 97203

Phone: +1 (805) 308-6503

SiaSands@hotmail.com

The information accessible from this book is for informational purposes only. None of the data within should be regarded as a promise of benefits, a statutory warranty, or a guarantee of results to be achieved.

Images are used under license from Fotosearch & Dreamstime.

Contents

Acknowledgment:

To my family, thank you for being there and accepting my wildness.

This book is dedicated to those with an open heart, an open mind, and a willingness to plumb the mysteries of life.

You make this world a better place.

Gemini 2021
Horoscope & Astrology

GEMINI

Gemini Dates: May 21 to June 21
Symbol: Twins
Element: Air
Planet: Mercury
House: Third
Colors: Yellow, blue

2021 inspires and delights with three gorgeous Supermoon's in the first half of the year, it is a time of fast-moving creativity and forward-thinking. There are some lovely changes set to flow into your life, something arrives, which makes you smile, it is going to let you step out of your ordinary routine and dive into a new area. The timing is ideal, this is a path which draws happiness and joy. It does show that your willingness to open your heart to a new level of potential does play a vital part in the events which unfold ahead. It is an enchanting chapter where you harness the magic within your spirit. It does set the tone of unique and inspiring options to be revealed in 2021.

On February 12^{th,} we ring in the Chinese New Year of the Ox, this is an important event, it brings grounded energy into your life. It is a time where you make progress on a personal goal; this draws stability into your life, it brings you to a path which draws happiness and excitement into your world. As you embark on a new adventure, you stoke the fires of your inspiration, creativity is a crucial element which provides solutions.

Mercury Retrograde gets up to tricks in 2021, taking time to nurture your spirit transports healing energy to your mind, body, and spirit. Information is revealed, which can be seen as being more critical than usual, it gives you a clue into the past, and this helps you gain insight into areas that have been troubling you. If you have been going through a difficult time, this information is the blueprint for future growth. It brings a theme of wellness to the surface that enables healing; it also brings closure and lets you finish chapters that feel done with.

Solar eclipses can only occur during a New Moon phase. This is when the Moon moves between Earth and the Sun, and these three celestial bodies form a straight line: Earth–Moon–Sun.

A Lunar eclipse occurs when the earth stands between the moon and the Sun, this obscures the light of the Sun from the moon. The moon herself has no light source of her own, as she simply reflects the light of the Sun. A lunar eclipse occurs during a Full Moon and usually marks endings, transitions, or other life cycle culmination points.

Any eclipse is a significant event in astrological circles, eclipses have fascinated scientists for centuries. Eclipses are dramatic tools that instigate change in your life. An eclipse is wild, free, expansive, and explosive, the wild cards of astrology, you never quite know what you get until it happens. An eclipse can uproot, surprise, inspire, motivate, and really become an active catalyst for change. Eclipses remove the shutters, they make you aware of areas that need to be changed and often spotlight an entirely new direction to explore. Eclipses inspire change and work rapidly to see forward motion occurring.

2021 delights with three gorgeous Supermoon's. A supermoon is when the moon is at its closest approach to Earth, which occurs during a full or new moon. The effect on the ocean's tides is most significant when there is a full or new moon. This tidal force is concentrated during the super moon, it can cause the ocean tides to rise by an extra inch or two compared to a regular full moon. Super moons are they invite you to look at your life, to reveal areas which you usually keep hidden. High in the night sky, they illuminate a great deal of information should you choose to work with this sacred energy. Connecting with this information gives you a fantastic opportunity to expand your life, to reveal areas that are ready to be developed.

As the moon peaks, it naturally begins to wane, and as the moon heads towards the next gravitational peak, the new moon phase, it has a cleansing effect on your emotional awareness. This helps you remove from your life all the things that need to be released, the areas which limit progress said no real good while they are kept within your spirit. Heading into the new moon gives your excellent opportunity to connect with the mysterious darkness. It is a healing time that brings a powerful sense of cleansing. This removes the outworn energy and makes space for new opportunities to flow into your world as the moon fills once again into a full shining globe.

PLANETARY RETROGRADES

The Retrograde phase is when a planet appears, when observed from Earth, to reverse direction. This happens due to an optical illusion caused by differences in orbit. The retrograde motion can have a negative influence on your life. The planet Mercury is the best-known planet for retrograde phases. This is because Mercury is the fastest planet in our solar system, and it enters a retrograde motion between three to four times a year, for about three weeks at a time. Mercury is a planet that rules communication, so you can expect frequent misunderstandings, scheduling problems, and disagreements during a Mercury Retrograde phase. Here is a quick reference guide to the retrogrades in 2021.

MERCURY: 3 RETROGRADES IN 2021

VENUS: 1 RETROGRADE IN 2021

MARS: NO RETROGRADE IN 2021

JUPITER: 1 RETROGRADE IN 2021

SATURN: 1 RETROGRADE IN 2021

URANUS: 2 RETROGRADE IN 2021

NEPTUNE: 1 RETROGRADE IN 2021

PLUTO: 1 RETROGRADE IN 2021

NODE: 1 RETROGRADE IN 2021

LILITH: NO RETROGRADE IN 2021

CHIRON: 1 RETROGRADE IN 2021

2021

Gemini Horoscope

Four Weeks Per Month

- Week 1 – Days 1 - 7
- Week 2 – Days 8 - 14
- Week 3 – Days 15 - 21
- Week 4 – Days 22 – Month-end

Time is set to Coordinated Universal Time Zone
(UT±0)

JANUARY ASTROLOGY

January 3, 4 - Quadrantids Meteor Shower.

The Quadrantids meteor shower run yearly from January 1-5. The Quadrantids meteor shower peaks this year on the night of the 3rd and morning of the 4th.

January 6 – Last Quarter Moon in Libra.

This Moon phase occurs at 09.37 UTC.

January 13 – New Moon in Capricorn.

This new moon phase occurs at 05:02 UTC. This cleans the slate and brings a fresh start. This is an excellent time to view galaxies and stars as there is no moonlight to obscure your view of the universe.

January 20 – First Quarter Moon in Aries.

This Moon phase occurs at 21.02 UTC.

January 24 – Mercury at Greatest Eastern Elongation.

The planet Mercury reaches greatest eastern elongation of 18.6 degrees from the Sun. This occurs at 02.00 UTC. Look for Mercury low in the sky just after sunset.

January 28 - Full Moon in Leo.

This phase occurs at 19:16 UTC. Full Wolf Moon. It has also been known as the Old Moon and the Moon After Yule. The Full Moon illuminates and draws new options to light.

January 29 – Jupiter in Conjunction with the Sun.

The planet Jupiter in Conjunction with the Sun. This occurs at 01:00 UTC.

January 30 – Mercury Retrograde begins in Aquarius.

During a retrograde period, it isn't the right time to move forward in any practical venture. Be prepared for misunderstandings and miscommunications to be prevalent.

The Quadrantids Meteor Shower blazes across the night sky this week. You reach a tipping point soon, which enables you to embrace a newfound flow of abundance. Information reaches you, which can be seen as a revelation. It does occur unexpectedly and may temporally blindside you as it's a big surprise at first. You need to think on your feet and come up with the best approach. It does push your boundaries back, but it could lead to the breakthrough you have been thinking about. Understanding the importance of this news does help you ascertain the right way to approach the situation. Information is revealed, which shines a light on new potential. It does see a significant change occurring, it involves an interpersonal bond. Someone in your life is ready to share their thoughts with you. It does bring a gift of abundance into your world. It brings a crossroads, and there can be one of two outcomes. A decision is required, it might see you need to regain your balance and think quickly on your feet.

Welcome news finally arrives, which sees life becoming more active. You begin to realize that you are much closer to achieving a long-held dream. You're getting close to a time that draws much abundance into your life. Information is shared that lights a path forward towards developing a new friendship and attending events that give you a chance to unwind and kick back with someone you feel understands you on a deeper level. It does bring socializing to the forefront, this information is big news, and it draws excitement into your world. It brings a new path to investigate.

The New Moon in Capricorn at the week's end brings a fork in the road soon, and decisive action may be necessary to achieve a lucrative new path. This week reminds you to remain mindful that finding the right way isn't an exact science. It is a process of refinement and exploration. Drawing new experiences into your world often provides learning and growth that is only understood in the rear vision mirror. Staying open to new avenues does crack open the potential possible. A bevy of enticing possibilities is ready to emerge to shift your focus forward. An option arrives that might cause you some consternation as it feels like a significant reach. You can handle growing your situation, and moving out of your comfort zone pushes back boundaries, it does become more comfortable once you adjust to new responsibilities. You will be amazed at how capable and productive you can be in this new role. Any issues that crop up are dealt with utilizing sterling creative solutions that come to mind. You are on the cusp of change when information arrives to provide clarity, it leads to a breakthrough moment. This secret reveals a gateway to a new chapter. It does have you think about the possibilities, this inspires you to reach for your vision. It does bring many benefits that accrue in your world, the more willing you are to open your heart, the more you stay in touch with developing your dreams. It seems that someone's real thoughts do show themselves when the secret information is revealed, knowing this person's feelings helps you make a decision. It's better to have an advance warning about this than to be kept in the dark. You have a remarkable ability to adapt and change to fit the circumstances.

This time speaks about changes occurring in your life soon. It will bring gifts that you can develop. Indeed, it gives you more insight into the path ahead, this provides clarity, it brings a sense of control over improving your situation. If you have been feeling uncertain about the right direction to cake take, it is a time that brings clarity. You dare to chase your dreams and excel. You may be tired of a situation that has been restricting your progress. Now is a time where you can rebel and break away from limitations. It requires innovative thinking, broadening your perception, and rethinking your strategy. You can create the change necessary to draw an exceptional path. It may see you diverging from your usual routine and entering a time of experimenting with new methods. Some big news is around the corner that is headline information. It reveals a blockbuster chapter is imminent. It brings exciting discussions, and it does offer you a more social aspect. You are ready to draw a new situation to light. A new friendship pours excitement onto the flames of your inspiration. A fateful moment brings a chapter connected with destiny. It gives you plenty to contemplate when this enticing secret reveals itself. It sees you going in strong and making strides on your goals. It's a time that rules identity, vision, and vitality. You begin a new chapter that offers you room to grow and advance your life. You intuitively know precisely the right elements to take in, and alternatively, the right areas to let go. Echoes of the past bring with them valuable insight. You face the decisions ahead with strength and determination. If you have felt yourself overthinking things, you can rest easy. It's merely a signpost from the divine, giving you a heads up.

Jupiter goes into Conjunction with the Sun the day after the Full Moon in Leo. Jupiter rules luck, growth, wisdom, and fortune. Life gets a boost from this cosmic alignment, it provides you with ample reason to celebrate. This week brings an essential shift forward that bolsters your potential. It does bring new options into your world, you discover a path opens that will likely grow your potential over the coming months. It is a sign that you are drawing the right journey to your life. It is an active and lively chapter; it resonates with a fresh start and epitomizes a new beginning. It leads to a happy time forward, a gateway to a bright future. You can continue to develop your experience following your core beliefs. Staying authentic and being true to yourself lets follow your vision correctly. It does bring new friendships and an improved situation to light. You are ready to begin a new cycle of life. If any areas have been causing delays, these are going to be left behind. You can create an environment that enables growth. A decision ahead draws a path that offers a wellspring of new ideas. It takes you to an actively creative place, you discover that your instinct is sharp and able to spotlight the right path to explore. This area is strongly associated with self-development. Improving your life is an essential focus. You may have some doubts in your mind, an introspective shift activates a pathway which enables you to ascertain the right direction to develop.

Mercury Retrograde begins in Aquarius at weeks end. You can navigate through this unsettling phase by keeping focused on the destination. Delay unnecessary deals, it's not the best time to sign any legal documents.

FEBRUARY ASTROLOGY

February 2 – Imbolc

Harness the element of fire to create something new. Inspiration, motivation, and creativity are rising. The earth is waking after winter's long sleep.

February 4 – Last Quarter Moon in Scorpio.

This Moon phase occurs at 17.37 UTC.

February 8 – Mercury at Inferior Conjunction.

The planet Mercury at Inferior Conjunction. This occurs at 14:00 UTC.

February 11 - New Moon in Aquarius.

This phase occurs at 19:06 UTC. This is an excellent time to view galaxies and stars as there is no moonlight to obscure your view of the universe. This is a time of rebirth and renewal. Create space for something new to arrive.

February 12 – Chinese New Year (Ox)

February 19 – First Quarter Moon in Taurus.

This Moon phase occurs at 18.47 UTC.

February 21 – Mercury Retrograde ends in Aquarius.

You can now move forward with any delayed plans that you have been putting off due to the Mercury Retrograde phase. Relationships should soon improve as miscommunications are overcome

February 27 - Full Moon in Virgo.

The Moon is on the opposite side of the Earth as the Sun and will be fully illuminated. This phase occurs at 08:17 UTC. This full moon is known as the Full Snow Moon. Powerful energy lights a path forward. You can attract and manifest excellent results during the complete moon phase.

There reasonable indications that an important decision is coming. Trusting in your intuition is the best bet. It does reveal full potential will soon emerge if you stay true to your instincts. A new day is dawning, and it's going to bring an original path to explore. There is a great deal of creativity emerging that sees more self-expression occurring, this places a strong focus on self-development. This speaks of change arriving. While this energy can feel disruptive, unsettling, and uncertain, you are going to create foundations that offer room to grow a path towards abundance. These changes are an essential element in increasing your situation, evolution is required to advance to your fullest potential. You are entering a fantastic time which sees the decks shuffled in your favor. It does bring new friendships that expand your circle. You begin to see a lot more progress in your life, there is an opportunity to socialize, and as you mingle and network with your more full social circle, you are the recipient of welcome news. It does see a conversation occurring that holds a big surprise, this reveal is something entirely unexpected, yet pleasing. It does take you towards developing a situation that you would like to keep under wraps, to begin with. It leaves you feeling excited and wanting to investigate a lead that holds promise. It's a significant chapter for you, you discover the universe is sending you a reminder to stay open to new options. If you have felt frustrated recently by a lack of progress in your personal life, this is set to change.

The New Moon this week does wipe the slate clean on many levels. Your life has undergone many changes, this can feel unsettling, but you have nailed the ability to make the most of the environment you find yourself in. Shuffling the deck of fate, you create an entirely new life path that resonates warmly. You can reap many benefits from expanding your life and experimenting with new modalities. The way ahead is exciting and adventurous. You may discover a whole new direction. Your situation is gathering speed, it does bring new people into your environment. This benefits your social life; you find out friends who inspire you to aim higher, they have similar interests, and you do have much in common with them. Getting involved in your wider community does bring a boost of good fortune, you are in line to reap an excellent harvest from networking and mingling with a diverse social circle. Unusual energy coming, which you can utilize as a dramatic tool to create progress and change in your life. It does alter your trajectory; it brings you towards a path that is more in keeping with where you hope to go. You can get busy and unpack a new chapter of potential. It does bring creativity to the forefront of your life. It's a fantastic shift forward. Exploring new options will bring an area that you can develop. Indeed, keeping your eyes open soon gives you more insight into the path ahead, being open to change gives a sense of control over improving your situation. If you have been feeling uncertain about the right direction to cake take, it is a time that brings clarity. You dare to chase your dreams and excel in an area that crosses your path soon.

Mercury Retrograde ends at weeks end. Life gives you a fantastic opportunity to utilize your creative side, and fan the flames of potential. It does leave you feeling inspired, you make strides on improving your situation, shaking off the doubt, connecting with the broader world of opportunity, you soon discover a path that offers room to grow your vision. It does draw happiness and abundance. Being open to change is a crucial element that enables you to pursue your goals. Your resilience and tenacity are heightened during this time. This gives you strength, it provides you with the confidence needed to step out of your usual demeanor and display the confidence needed to expand your life. It does set the tone for developing a presence on your terms, as you grow the barriers of your life, it does draw a happier chapter, and this is a critical shift forward for you. There is a message arriving to get you thinking about the potential possible in your life. It does pay to look at the bigger picture, expand your mind and your belief systems. You are capable of manifesting an exact situation that draws happiness into your world. It is a time that sees a powerful shift occurring; this contributes to new options, it sets a trend that brings growth, and this helps you go after your goals. It enables you to see progress occurring reasonably quickly. Advancing your situation blazes a new path forward. Your creative thinking is going to spotlight a new option to explore soon.

The Full Moon in Virgo occurs this week, this can create energy peaks that illuminate and draw clarity. You may be questioning the path ahead and trying to ascertain the right area to fully develop. There is an essence of trial and error to this process, not every option is going to stick. However, being open to new avenues does begin to draw the right situation to light. It brings something that turns out to be a significant boost. It does attract the success you seek into your world. You discover this is something that can be expanded and built upon. This all goes very well for you, and this leads to a busy time, it does see headway occurring around some of your larger goals. Things don't land in your lap without the effort being expended to make things happen, expanding your horizons is the ticket to success. It sees you operating efficiently and at an energetic level. It does let you dive in and enjoy a bounty of new experiences.

Utilizing innovative methods to improve your situation is sufficient. You create a firm foundation that can be built upon. Robust accomplishments complement your hard work. Life supports growth and productivity, it is a time of setting the bar higher and achieving results that bring your talents to a new level. There is something in the pipeline that hits the sweet spot and leaves you feeling inspired to try a new direction. You begin to feel inspired again, this gets you ready to plan the moves, which can increase the potential possible in your world. Pressing forward towards obtaining your vision, lets you be proactive about getting top results. This is a time of transitions, the winds of change blow in, and they carry you towards new foundations.

March 6 - Mercury Greatest Elongation.

The planet Mercury reaches its greatest elongation of 27.3 degrees from the Sun. If you would like to view Mercury, look for Mercury low in the eastern sky just before sunrise.

March 6 – Last Quarter Moon in Sagittarius.

This Moon phase occurs at 01.30 UTC. –

March 11 – Neptune in Conjunction with the Sun.

The planet Neptune in Conjunction with the Sun. This occurs at 00:00 UTC.

March 13 - New Moon in Pisces.

The New Moon creates space for a new chapter. This phase occurs at 10:21 UTC. This is an excellent time to observe galaxies and stars because there is no moonlight to obscure your view of the universe.

March 20 - Vernal Equinox.

The March equinox takes place at 09:37 UTC. There are equal amounts of day and night throughout the world.

March 21 – First Quarter Moon in Gemini.

This Moon phase occurs at 14.40 UTC.

March 26 - Venus Superior Conjunction.

The planet Venus at Superior Conjunction. This occurs at 06:00 UTC.

March 28 - Full Moon in Libra.

This Moon is on the opposite side of the Earth as the Sun and shall be fully illuminated. This phase occurs at 18:48 UTC. This full moon is known as the Full Worm Moon. Powerful energy lights a path forward. You can attract and manifest excellent results during the complete moon phase.

Mercury reaches greatest elongation this week. This can feel destabilizing, but in fact, it creates a useful change, you move away from destructive influences and create lifestyle changes that draw benefits. This is a time that brings new options into your world. There is an emphasis on advancing a goal, and it does kick off a favorable chapter, which lets you create a fresh start. You may discover a curious direction that inspires your mind, it does connect you to like-minded people, and this sees an open door towards a more social environment. It does have a positive ripple effect, drawing new friendships. Setting appropriate boundaries creates the right environment that enables you to discover your truest tribe, and it lets you move forward towards an essential group endeavor. You may see some alliances shifting, and this draws emphasis on improving bonds with those who support you the most. Applying lessons learned previously is the ticket to success. It does bring new foundations that grow your potential. Life brings an unexpected boost soon. While this surprise may feel random, it is a sign that you are on the right track to developing your life. If you have felt unsettled recently and found yourself dealing with extra stress, this news is set to bring new joy into your world. It does introduce you to friendly people who share similar ideas and interests, a new trend is ready to blossom. A new trend is ready to emerge, it does bring an energy that is quite liberating and refreshing. A new friendship springs to life, it does kick off a trend of improving your social circle.

Neptune arrives in conjunction with the Sun this week. The Planet Neptune rules dreams and healing, while the Sun places a strong focus on self-development and improvement. This can usher in many changes. It does definitely grow your potential, the influence of the Sun draws an energizing power that bolsters your spirit. You're ready to turn over a new page, something is refreshing in the wind that is going to flow into your world soon. It does, in essence, bring a new dawn. It is a time that lets your creativity fly free and soar high. You launch towards a path that builds a foundation, you can expand. Staying true to your inner voice culminates in an authentic vision. Information arrives that brings a meaningful project to light. It pushes your talents. It ascends your abilities, and it does have you thinking big about the next steps to take. This news, in essence, offers a gateway towards growth. It does bring loads of activity, and it has you feeling highly creative. You share thoughts and ideas with a close confidant, this brings to light an incredible epiphany. Life holds a refreshing twist when surprise news reaches you soon. It does bring a fast-paced environment, you forge ahead towards achieving your goals. Unscrambling this information does offer a side path to explore. It brings a grand plan into focus, this avenue is ambitious, it brings a success-driven chapter. You get an idea of the right direction, this relates to revealing your life purpose.

Additionally, the New Moon in Pisces this week sees some unusual changes are occurring. It primarily draws an environment that is healing and abundant. Intentions are set at this time, go far, and you see a goal reach fruition the next full moon.

Ostara, the Spring Equinox, takes center stage this week. It's all about facing the sun again after the long winter and starting new plans and goals, you can harvest later in the year. You weave a spell of manifestation; it draws exciting new options into your life. This Spring Equinox speaks about the opportunities coming into your life soon. You will be the beneficiary of new possibilities, an original path opens and brings plenty of golden energy into your life. You can have high hopes as excitement is set to shine in your world. It does bring new people, circulating in your wider community offers room to grow your life. Things are ready to shift forward. An area you push forward toward does draw dividends. It does bring productivity, and in this busyness, you thrive. Your creativity is rising, and this could see a project you get involved with reach a new level. It brings an aspect that enables you to draw the magic into your life and manifest a rewarding outcome. Your tried and true methods are a highway to success. You work hard and have much to show for your efforts, now you are ready to crank up the potential possible, and an area makes itself known; it is a perfect fit. The timing is intriguing, as it feels like it is tailor-made for your talents. It gives you the right avenue to press forward in and expand your horizons. Things develop and begin to take shape with this curious venture. The time is ripe to go after your goals. Trusting the universe to support your expansion, you can take flight and seek a path that draws abundance into your life. You do find an area which stokes the fires of your imagination, this has you dreaming big about future goals, it does land you in an area which is ready for your talents.

Venus sashays into your life this week. A positive influence flows into your life, it brings enriching life experiences and underscores an atmosphere of change, harmony, and joy. You become more confident about moving out of your comfort zone and seeking out your tribe of kindred spirits. You benefit from a more active environment, this lines up an avenue that has you meeting new people. Suddenly, your circle of friends grows, and you are happy to see modern influences arriving. Talks ahead reveal enticing information. It does see you motivated to pursue your goals, you connect with passion, and add a dash of a manifestation to the mix. It brings rejuvenation and offers a bountiful path towards new goals. Lively discussions strengthen interpersonal bonds, you find yourself working as part of a team. This social aspect draws well-being as bonds spring to life. News arrives that deserves your undivided attention. You have good reason to celebrate, it does bring an offer that feels like a perfect fit. You embrace a new chapter that leads to pursuing your dreams. It paints a picture of fantastic growth being possible, advancing your potential brings a breakthrough moment. You feel inspired and think outside the box when it comes to planning a path forward.

Additionally, the Full Moon in Libra highlights a time of increasing opportunity, a major makeover is coming. The exciting news is coming soon, it is a game-changing chapter, you are given room to expand your situation by focusing your energy on developing an area which captures your imagination. You have a natural knack for unveiling the highest potential possible in any given case.

April 4 – Last Quarter Moon in Capricorn.

This Moon phase occurs at 10.02 UTC.

April 12 - New Moon in Aries.

The New Moon phase occurs at 2:31 UTC. This is an excellent time to observe galaxies and stars because there is no moonlight visible.

April 19 – Mercury at Superior Conjunction.

The planet Mercury at Superior Conjunction. This occurs at 02:00 UTC.

April 20 – First Quarter Moon in Leo.

This Moon phase occurs at 06.59 UTC.

April 22, 23 - Lyrids Meteor Shower.

The Lyrids meteor shower runs each year from April 16-25. This meteor shower peaks on the night of the 22nd and the morning of the 23rd. These meteors can produce bright dust trails that last for several seconds.

April 27 - Full Moon in Scorpio, Supermoon.

The Moon is on the opposite side of the Earth as the Sun and will be completely illuminated. Full Pink Moon. It's the first of three supermoons for 2021. This occurs at 03:31 UTC. The Moon will be at its closest approach to the Earth and may look slightly larger and brighter than usual. Powerful energy lights a path forward. You can attract and manifest excellent results during the full moon phase.

April 30 – Uranus in Conjunction with the Sun.

The planet Uranus in Conjunction with the Sun. This occurs at 21:00 UTC.

Revolutionary changes are transitioning you forward. This lets you break free from the past, you light up a new pathway, it revamps your potential. Restoration of spirit motivates you to chase your dreams. It does bring a new option to contemplate. As you reach a new frontier, this open territory offers a clean slate potential. It is representative of a more general theme of abundance which has been seeking to tempt you forward recently. Your ability to navigate complexities and come out on top does draw new options into your world. Your resilience and perseverance revamp your trajectory, it does bring a brighter chapter. You reach the completion of a significant journey, and as the cycle reboots, you plot a new section. It does see firm foundations being set, bringing with it an enriching and abundant path forward. Reflection and contemplation draw insight and wisdom. All is revealed soon when a secret is revealed. It does enable you to make progress in a personal area. Things are coming together nicely, it draws a journey of meaningful conversations, and opens a gateway towards improving the stability possible in your world. It depicts a pivotal time where you prioritize the development of your dreams. Being proactive about what you seek brings tangible results, improvements soon follow. Urgent news arrives to tempt you forward. Your prospects are rising, and an area you discover around the corner draws a new option to light. It does bring with it a flurry of activity that is exciting. An upgrade is coming, which sees your situation evolving; it does let you overcome blocks and takes you toward a winning path.

The New Moon in Aries packs a nugget of wisdom. It is a time of excitement, inspiration, and creativity, it does have you dreaming big about future goals. Your life is one of exploration, you are someone who has an exceptional ability to remove barriers and seek a higher path. You can set your sights on your brightest goals, something that is begun soon will reach fruition at years end. An open road of potential tempts you forward, focusing on your priorities brings the kind of advancement that keeps the fires of motivation burning. A new adventure calls your name soon enough, it does bring sunshine after rain. Something you let go of does return differently. Inspiration sweeps into your life, it brings a pathway that fuels your heart and mind. Someone you encounter plays an integral part in the events ahead. There is an emphasis on emotional wellness, a brave decision sees you pushing back barriers to chase your dreams. The challenges you have faced have made you stronger. It does bring personal growth, distilling this energy down into its most pure form creates a spark of inspiration. It brings courage, it creates change. A whole new path is awaiting your open heart. You crack the code and discover an area that brings real meaning into your life, it does see a meeting of the minds occur with a kindred spirit. Some significant changes are happening, and this relates to following a path that enables you to connect with your more profound vision. You cross the road of an individual who inspires your mind. This becomes a portal to a happier chapter, it brings a more conscious environment where you dive into self-expression, meaningful conversations, and sharing of thoughts and ideas with someone who understands.

Mercury at Superior conjunction this week sees you reaching a crossroads, it can be challenging to know the path ahead when you face a dissecting road. A refreshing twist ignites your creativity. It brings smoldering energy, which enables you to get an idea of where you're headed before you set the situation ablaze. It does see changes occurring in your life that sparks a confident new chapter. It removes any energy that's past its expiration date, and this flicks open a fresh start that inspires healing. You discover one who sparks your interest and takes a bold step towards your vision. You are ready to create exceptional growth that touches all areas of your life. The first step is being open to new experiences, keep your energy upbeat and positive lets you surround yourself with people who also support your growth. As you ascend and advance your situation, you land gently in an environment that brings new adventures to explore. It takes you to an abundant path that may involve a leap of faith forward. Life holds a refreshing twist soon. It does remove the edge off things, a new flow of abundance enters your world. It brings more stability and tempts you forward towards a path of inspiration. You set your life ablaze with new options, it is just the avenue you were seeking. It brings a valuable shift forward, which is healing and therapeutic.

News arrives, which ushers in a new chapter. A significant situation is coming, as you stand on the precipice of change, it is beneficial to reflect and release any unresolved energy that could be holding you back from a new chapter of potential. Your heart guides you, bringing an essential shift forward. You discover you can set your sights on long-term goals.

The Full Moon in Scorpio is a Supermoon that sweeps into your life to draw closure, healing, and this transitions you forward. There is a mystery surrounding you; something you seek is going to be revealed. It does bring a moment of clarity, which helps shift your plan towards strategy and creating the action steps to achieve your dreams. Wishful thinking is all excellent, but taking proactive measures is the necessary follow-up to manifest your goals. You are ready to take the next step forward. You get some help that helps you make an important decision. The events that follow unfold in a manner that brings you to a new direction. It does let an exciting area to make a dramatic flourish in your life. This is a time of creating change, a gateway forward, and the beginning of a new cycle. A moment ahead triggers a sudden shift forward. It does begin a journey that increases stability and has you scouting new options. It does initiate a flurry of changes around love, friendship, and meaningful bonds. The essential lessons of the past enable you to go into the next chapter with your eyes open. It does bring a relationship to light that offers you room to plot a course towards your vision. It brings long discussions, and you get an idea of what may be possible through being willing to open your heart to another who has also overcome challenges. It takes you towards a new chapter, a shift forward sees a broader perspective arrive. It unfolds gently, letting you process all that has gone before. As you dip your toes into a new situation, you begin to see fresh possibilities that leave you feeling starry-eyed. It brings a transit forward with one who is attentive, this person is a good listener and understands life.

May 3 – Last Quarter Moon in Aquarius.

This Moon phase occurs at 17.50 UTC.

May 6, 7 - Eta Aquarids Meteor Shower.

The Eta Aquarids meteor shower runs annually from April 19 to May 28. It peaks this year on the night of May 6 and the morning of May 7.

May 11 - New Moon in Taurus.

This phase occurs at 19:00 UTC. The new moon phase is a brilliant time to observe galaxies and stars because there is no moonlight visible.

March 17 - Mercury Greatest Eastern Elongation.

The planet Mercury reaches its greatest eastern elongation of 22 degrees from the Sun. If you would like to view Mercury, look for the Mercury low in the sky just after sunset. This planetary phase occurs at 06.00 UTC.

May 19 – First Quarter Moon in Virgo.

This Moon phase occurs at 19.13 UTC.

May 26 - Full Moon in Sagittarius, Supermoon.

This phase occurs at 11:14 UTC. Full Flower Moon. It's the second of three supermoons for 2021. The Moon will be at its closest approach to the Earth and may look slightly larger and brighter than usual. Powerful energy lights a path forward. You can attract and manifest excellent results during the full moon phase.

May 26 – Total Lunar Eclipse in Sagittarius.

A total lunar eclipse occurs when the Moon passes completely through the Earth's dark shadow or umbra. During this type of eclipse, the Moon gradually gets more mysterious and then take on a rusty or blood red color. This eclipse occurs at 11:19 UTC.

May 29 – Mercury Retrograde begins in Gemini.

During a retrograde period, it isn't the right time to move forward in any practical venture. Be prepared for misunderstandings and miscommunications to be prevalent.

There is a cluster of activity coming into your life, which leaves you feeling exuberant. This expansiveness does spark your curiosity; it has you sorting through several options and launching towards a phase of growth and good fortune. It does take your ambitions to a higher trajectory, switching into high gear is the perfect fuel for your inspiration. You are working hard to break fresh ground in your career. It does bring transformation, your intentions draw a path that offers room to progress your vision. Gaining traction in a new area does bring growth. Staying focused, you can plot a course that advances your situation. It brings an inspirational adventure, it begins with an offer that arrives to tempt you to a new role. This relates to stepping into your own authority in the workplace. It speaks of a new option coming soon. It does bring new responsibilities and learning, you are ready to crack open this chapter and dive deeply into an area that calls your name. It does see you focused on achieving your mission, nothing breaks your stride. Giving your all is the ticket to success. This tunnel vision is what is required to make your dream a reality. Stability is on the rise, it lands you in an environment that enables you to grow your situation. Something you've been working on does take flight, this lights the way forward. You are ready to swap self-defeating patents for new methods, don't buy into doubt, you know you can achieve a stellar outcome if you stay true to your spirit. You have worked hard to create a firm foundation; this is fundamental to attain growth. You soon complete an important goal that enables you to progress your situation.

The Taurus New Moon this week says that it's out with the old and in with the new. This is a time where your feelings may fluctuate if you feel sensitive or triggered by any issues, take time to focus on nurturing your spirit. Fortifying your foundations brings grounded and balanced energy, which hits the sweet spot for your environment. Self-development is likely to come into focus, it brings a self-expressive and creative path towards abundance.

There are changes afoot, which correspond with developing your personal life. It does rule time of increasing your options, and this opens a door towards a vital conversation that sparks up a situation worthy of investigation. Developing a bond with someone of interest does see you branch out and enjoy new experiences. It may even prompt an exciting trip away to an exotic destination. The wheels are in motion to draw a happier chapter, in essence, a great deal of healing occurs between you both. It does enable you to plot a course towards a more stable landscape. It is a time that releases the blockages and creates space for more harmony to emerge. There is something in the pipeline that brings new potential into your life. It does bring change, releasing areas that did not reach full potential creates space for something new to blossom. It is an enriching chapter, you plot a course towards developing a long-term vision. A flow of harmony and abundance supports a phase of growth and romance. You make headway on improving a situation that inspires your mind.

Mercury reaches greatest elongation from the Sun this week. This reveals that you are positioned to advance your life. It centers on developing a situation that brings magical potential into your world. You are right to be curious and investigate leads, expanding your horizons is going to carry a new mission. Ask questions, look at new options, and continue to grow your world. You can achieve a great deal by being proactive and advancing your situation each and every day. A path is opening for you soon, you are ready to strengthen your position and build a firm foundation that creates the basis for future growth. Capitalizing on your talents is a critical ingredient that nixes doubt and blends your gifts to cook up a storm. New potential tempts you forward, it does expand your boundaries, learning and growth add the right dash of spice to your life. An invitation sees you circulating in a new environment. A fantastic message could arrive shortly, it does shine a light on improved communication in a social setting. It brings long-awaited news, and this promotes growth. It sets the stage for a meaningful moment to crack open a new chapter of potential. It does see a deep commitment to a personal goal take center stage. It brings enthusiasm, which empowers you to take the next step forward. An enchanting possibility hangs in the air. Your life hasn't been an easy one. A piece of the puzzle being revealed soon. It does bring clarity, releasing past blockages, it helps you make the correct choice for your situation. You soon enter a landscape ripe with potentiality. Advancing your position puts you in the box seat to obtain stellar growth. It opens the door to a brighter section, one that is dynamic and evolving.

This week delivers a plethora of cosmic activity. There is a full moon in Sagittarius, which is also a super moon, and on the same night, a total lunar eclipse. This is a triple magnifying event. But be warned, three days later Mercury retrograde begins in Gemini, this is the mule kick that may just knock you sideways if you're not aware, that it is coming. So what does all this mean for your life? The triple combo event on Wednesday brings changes that spark a new path. You should seek new experiences and keep open to learning areas that trigger your intuition. Unexpected events sparking enlightenment, it brings a whole new track, you tap into a more creative environment, you share your gifts with others. It does activate a path that harnesses artistic or innovative ideas to give back to a broader community. Tapping into an established knowledge base will also bring new information to light that could spark a revolution in your world. As you adopt a new trajectory, you discover new friends who support your personal growth. It does see you taking more of an active part in your local community. There is a transit occurring which takes you to a new chapter, this shakes up your world, it offers options to see you excel in your chosen endeavor. Your pioneering spirit is boosted by events on the horizon, it does bring harmony, a wide-open road beckons. Information arrives soon, which sends you on a mission to seek further knowledge. It does turn your situation on its head. Broadening your perception opens a new pathway towards growth. An exchange ahead makes a powerful statement to another. You step into your own authority, and take on a leadership role, sharing your gifts with a broader audience.

June 2 – Last Quarter Moon in Pisces.

This Moon phase occurs at 07.24 UTC.

June 10 - New Moon in Gemini.

This moon phase occurs at 10:53 UTC. This is an excellent time to observe galaxies and stars because there is little moonlight to obstruct your view.

June 10 – Annual Solar Eclipse.

An annular solar eclipse occurs when the Moon is too far away from the Earth to completely cover the Sun, it results in a ring of light around the dark Moon. The Sun's corona isn't visible during an annular eclipse. This solar eclipse is visible in eastern Russia, the Arctic Ocean, western Greenland, and Canada. A partial eclipse will be visible in the northeastern United States, Europe, and most of Russia. This eclipse occurs at 10.42 UTC.

June 11 – Mercury at Inferior Conjunction.

The planet Mercury at Inferior Conjunction. This occurs at 01:00 UTC.

June 18 – First Quarter Moon in Libra.

This Moon phase occurs at 03.54 UTC.

June 21 - June Solstice.

The June solstice occurs at 03:32 UTC. The North Pole will be tilted toward the Sun, which, having reached its northernmost position in the sky, will be over the Tropic of Cancer at 23.44 degrees north latitude. This heralds the first day of summer (summer solstice) in the Northern Hemisphere, the summer solstice is considered one of the most important times of the year for many traditional cultures.

June 22 – Mercury Retrograde ends in Gemini.

You can now move forward with any delayed plans that you have been putting off due to the Mercury Retrograde phase. Relationships should soon improve as miscommunications are overcome

June 24 - Full Moon in Capricorn, Supermoon.

The Moons will be completely illuminated. This moon phase occurs at 18:40 UTC. Full Strawberry Moon. This is the last of three supermoons for 2021. The Moon will be at its closest approach to the Earth and may look slightly larger and brighter than usual. Powerful energy lights a path forward. You can attract and manifest excellent results during the full moon phase.

You have the stamina to stay on top of things during this Mercury Retrograde phase. You may face some current hurdles soon, the path ahead is tricky to negotiate. You have met this environment before, and you do your best to deal with the issues as they arrive. Options are coming to improve your love life, essential changes see refreshing energy blowing into your world. It does help your situation shift towards a more harmonious phase. Looking at the past provides you with valuable insight, you can see how your life has transformed over time. You are now ready to embrace the new potential. A restless spirit thrives in a busy and curious environment. As you expand your horizons, you discover a situation that offers a path towards a happy time. It does see, your confidence is on the rise and leading you towards a major turning point. You are set to benefit from news, which provides you with insight into your situation. It does enable you to capitalize on fresh energy; it puts you in the box seat to land in an environment which is ripe for new potential. It does take time to heal the past, but the inner work you do does kick off a bountiful cycle which orients you towards a time of renewal. It is the beginning of a new journey that takes you far. This news does motivate and inspires you to strive to better your circumstances. Finding the right direction to feel passionate about enables you to break the rules and reveal an exciting chapter, which is likely to play a prominent part in the next aspect of your life. This takes you to a vital time, which is liberating and freewheeling. You embrace a shift forward and land gently in a new area.

The New Moon in Gemini combines with an annular solar eclipse, this sees change ahead for you. You face a crossroads, and there is a decision arriving soon, which is a gateway to a happy chapter. Once you cross through this portal, you discover an option that burns brightly. Groundbreaking potential flows into your life to inspire your mind. There are many aspects of this environment, which capture the essence of creativity, it launches a fresh start and enables you to set sail towards a vision of your own making. It does take you towards a significant time where you can embrace developing your intuition. Exciting news arrives, which can be seen as a signpost. In fact, it does bring an essential shift forward. There are changes ahead for your life path, it has you feeling happy and enthusiastic as you become involved in learning a new area of interest. This beautifully aligns you towards growth, it has you merging with other successful types, and this brings remarkable stability into your world. You have worked hard to achieve the rewards which currently surround you. An avenue you explore helps you move forward with purposefulness. It does bring the sparkle into your world. The seeds planted during this phase ripen into a beautiful harvest. You are wrapping up a vital cycle, preparing to embark on a new journey that will take you forward. Taking a deep breath, reviewing your progress, releasing areas that have no relevance in your future vision will enable you to make the right step towards achieving your goals You can create the change you are seeking. Taking a bold move forward, you make a decision that has a substantial impact on your life in the chapter ahead. There is magic in expanding your horizons.

The June 21st Solstice at weeks end is an ideal time to reflect on your goals. There is a new chapter coming which beckons and calls your name. You enter an energizing phase, which enables you to create essential changes. This resets your potential, it offers you a path towards developing an area that inspires your mind and cultivates your creative side. It does see you becoming more involved with a trail of passion. Shaking off any lingering doubts, you embrace a shift forward towards the realization of a long-held goal. You are transitioning towards new opportunities, and it sees you remove limitations that currently hold progress back. Once these restrictions are lifted, you get a sense of a path that brings growth and stability. It aligns you towards a direction that brings fundamental changes around some of your larger goals. Your instincts are sharpened, ready to spot an opportunity that crosses your path. It does see essential changes occurring to bring harmony to the forefront of your life. It really energizes your social life and brings welcome news. Change, revolution, and innovation are at the crux of improving your situation. It brings a pioneering time that is adventurous and expansive. If there is any area of your life that has failed to reach its actual potential, you soon discover a mission that brings new options to contemplate. This news turns your perceptions upside down. It may be seen as highly controversial, and it does incite change; it brings a path that pushes you to expand your boundaries. Broadening your scope, you leave previous assumptions in the dust of the past. Enlightenment draws a whole new track, this has you getting involved with a diverse and eclectic social circle. It is a highly creative time that sweeps in a revolutionary potential.

Mercury Retrograde ends this week. Memories of the past may be tugging on your awareness to encourage you to pause and reflect. This creates space to resolve any residual feelings that may be clinging to your spirit and limiting growth. Addressing sensitive areas does trigger the first phase of potential. You have been going through some changes, it does give you a snapshot of your more exceptional abilities. You rise up to meet challenges, you discover new pathways towards growth, he admires your innovation, your tenacity, and, most importantly, your resilience. There is an avenue open that draws further information, leading to a path that turns the volume up on your potential. It brings a greater sense of purpose. News arrives, which tempts you towards an exciting new area. It fits the bill for your current framework, it takes you forward. Learning the lessons of the past triggers a whole original path. It is a journey that takes your talents further. Still, in the short term, it's likely to be a balancing act. You have innovative and artistic ideas to explore, a situation you become involved in sparks a revolution of potential. It does bring a lively journey that offers you room to grow your world. It lands you in a comfortable position, your consistency and dedication draw dividends. It is a busy time that focuses on developing your goals. You hear exciting news about a career option; it does bring information that captures your attention and enables you to plot a course forward. This work is regular, stable, and rewarding. It provides you with tangible results, and you feel a sense of accomplishment, as things come together nicely. It does have you feeling appreciated for your efforts, it builds the right foundations for you.

July 1 – Last Quarter Moon in Aries.

This Moon phase occurs at 21.11 UTC.

July 4 - Mercury at Greatest Western Elongation.

The planet Mercury reaches greatest western elongation of 20.6 degrees from the Sun. If you would like to view Mercury, look for Mercury low in the eastern sky just before sunrise. This planetary phase occurs at 20.00 UTC.

July 10 - New Moon in Cancer.

The New Moon draws rebirth and new energy. This moon phase occurs at 01:17 UTC. This is an excellent time to observe galaxies and stars because there is no moonlight visible.

July 17 – First Quarter Moon in Libra.

This Moon phase occurs at 10.11 UTC.

July 24 - Full Moon in Aquarius.

The Moon is located on the opposite side of the Earth as the Sun and will be fully illuminated. This phase occurs at 02:37 UTC. This full moon is known as Full Buck Moon. Powerful energy lights a path forward. You can attract and manifest excellent results during the complete moon phase.

July 28, 29 - Delta Aquarids Meteor Shower.

The Delta Aquarids meteor shower peaks on the night of July 28 and the morning of July 29. The first quarter moon may block many of the fainter meteors this year. You should still be able to view some brighter ones. Best views should occur after midnight. Meteors radiate from the constellation Aquarius but may appear anywhere in the sky.

July 31 – Last Quarter Moon in Taurus.

This Moon phase occurs at 13.16 UTC.

Mercury at Greatest elongation this week brings unique vibrations. Something arrives, which is a culmination of a project, it is a matter involving business, it appears that you are now ready to reach for more. An opportunity that has been in the pipeline for some time does make itself known. Your diligence and productivity impress a decision-maker who takes your talents into consideration when offering you this new role. It may take your plan to new heights, a monumental path opens, this activates your ambitious side. Ratcheting up the potential does see you make headway towards an ambitious goal. It is a venture that could rapidly develop soon. This enterprise draws dividends, it does recognize your energy focused on a refreshing area and harnesses your talents to good effect. It brings new adventures and growth, exploring the opportunities ahead helps you stretch beyond your current boundaries. A visionary Avenue entices you to think big about developing entrepreneurial ideas, your creativity and innovation are sparked. Information reaches you that brings a path of evolution. It does see an option arriving that tempts you to become more expressive. It brings a welcome distraction, you focus on developing an area that is trailblazing and creative. It does see significant headway being made towards a vision that inspires you. A growth opportunity is a seed that is planted, your aspirations, and dedication brings tangible results. You soon discover something on offer that holds value. It gives you an inkling of how things are going to progress.

The New Moon in Cancer this week signifies a new beginning. News arrives, which initiates a wave of potential flowing into your world. It brings transformation, a breakthrough moment is imminent. It does bring a highly creative journey, you blend ideas and come up with a path that is off the beaten track. This new trajectory does give you broader options, it utilizes your gifts to full effect. As you lay the groundwork, you build a foundation that offers you room to grow and prosper. It is a significant time, your gut feeling is that this information is worth exploring further. You relish the challenge, it brings a new option to your table. This is a gateway towards a happier phase of developing your abilities and striking out in an area that is inspiring. It brings moments to treasure and draws abundance, exploring this potential, lightens your spirit, and brings the magic back. If you have found yourself feeling restless recently, you will appreciate the changes ahead. It does provide a clear incentive to try new options. A great deal of proactive energy is coming to shift your focus forwards. This news arrives out of the blue and inspires a phase of growth. You enter a busy time that utilizes your creative abilities. The sharing of thoughts and ideas with others creates an excellent brew of potential. You discover that fortune favors the bold. It brings an auspicious time, which expands your horizons. An offer crosses your path, and this plants the seeds, which in time will harvest into a bumper crop of abundance. There's a great deal of activity coming, it brings a journey of growth and learning. This brings change, it illuminates an option that reinvigorates your spirit as you step forward into the next chapter of life.

An opportunity that supports your vision emerges, this brings terrific advancement. It marks a chapter where change is possible. You discover that expanding your horizons draws new options. Life supports your growth; it rules the time of creative thinking, adventure, and productivity. Manoeuvering forward, you embrace a landscape that is highlighted by increasing abundance. It's a delightful shift forward toward your goals. You have specific goals in mind, you are soon allowed to press forward and launch toward an area that offers you room to grow your situation. It does bring an abundance of potential, you discover you can step into your own authority, you embrace following your heart and enjoy a more creative and expressive chapter. It's a time of sweeping away areas that no longer appeal and reaching for your dreams. You are ready to create an abundant pathway to success. You are entering a time of transformation, it brings potent options into your world. Essentially, you wipe the slate clean and begin a fresh chapter. It brings something new and exciting, good fortune accompanies you on this journey forward. News arrives, which has you thinking about the possibilities. Whatever comes and goes, it's going to work out for the best. You can set the bar high and achieve a positive outcome. You may find things smooth over reasonably well, a time of contemplation draws new solutions. It can feel intense, but it does lead to the renewal of spirit. Some curious aspects are likely to emerge in your life, which gets you more involved in learning and developing your talents. New concepts and ideas flow into your world, it brings refreshing options, and this also draws new friendships.

The magic of the Full Moon arrives to put you in manifestation mode. Things are on the move, there is a shift forward soon that is a source of inspiration. It marks a bold new beginning and sets you on a path of new possibilities. Your willingness to harness a sense of adventure and initiate change draws luck and good fortune. It is a time that brings new foundations and jump-starts a journey that draws dividends. Life shimmers with new possibilities, a venture you become involved with is a raging success. It does take your motivation further, and this enables you to excel. The more you develop your ideas, the higher your vision takes you. Your creativity merges with an innovative type, it brings a bonding session and lively discussions. You get off the revolving door and discover a path that can be grown into an enterprising success. Finding the right trajectory brings your career to a new level. It gives you a project that you can sink your teeth into, a new role offers fresh possibilities. It is an area that has plenty of room to grow your talents. Seeing rewards for the work undertaken draws fresh inspiration, it brings a productive and active cycle to light. A turning point arrives soon, it gives you permission to follow your dreams and chase your vision. Abundance and happiness become a focal point, you use this tunnel vision to create the lifestyle changes necessary that draw joy into your world. It does see you becoming in sync with your creative vision, and an opportunity ahead triggers a new path towards success. It brings a necessary transition and gets the ball rolling towards growth. It sees an outpouring of creativity is possible, an endeavor you focus on does take flight, you watch your ideas blossom.

AUGUST ASTROLOGY

August 1 – Mercury at Superior Conjunction.

The planet Mercury at Superior Conjunction. This planetary event occurs at 14:00 UTC.

August 2 - Saturn at Opposition.

The beautiful ringed planet Saturn will be at its nearest approach to Earth and will be illuminated by the Sun. This planetary event occurs at 05:00 UTC.

August 8 - New Moon in Leo.

This moon phase occurs at 13:50 UTC. This is an excellent time to observe galaxies and stars because there is no moonlight to obstruct the view. A new chapter awaits an open heart.

August 12, 13 - Perseids Meteor Shower.

The Perseids meteor shower runs each year from July 17 to August 24. It peaks this year on the night of August 12 and the morning of August 13. The Perseids meteor shower is usually excellent viewing as the meteors are so bright and numerous. The moon sets early in the evening, leaving dark skies for what could be a unique show. The best viewing is from after midnight.

August 15 – First Quarter Moon in Scorpio.

This Moon phase occurs at 15.20 UTC.

August 19 - Jupiter at Opposition.

The Giant planet Jupiter will be at its nearest approach to Earth and will be at it's brightest. This planetary event occurs at 23:00 UTC.

August 22 - Full Moon in Aquarius, Blue Moon.

The Full Moon draws clarity and illumination. This phase occurs at 12:02 UTC. Full Sturgeon Moon. This year it is also a blue moon. This event only happens on average once every 2.7 years, giving rise to the term, "once in a blue moon." There are three full moons in each season of the year. But as full moons occur every 29.53 days, occasionally a season contains 4 full moons. The additional full moon of the season is known as a blue moon.

August 30 – Last Quarter Moon in Gemini.

This Moon phase occurs at 07.13 UTC.

Saturn at opposition this week brings the energy that is diligent, persevering, reliable, stable, patient. It lets you possess the ability to concentrate. You get off to a fabulous start when an opportunity crosses your path. It does see you merging your talents with an innovative business idea. It brings a new chapter, and this is a source of inspiration. A bold new beginning has you on a path of exploration. Investing your energy wisely, you focus on developing an area that offers room to grow and prosper. A smart and insightful person with a sunny disposition enters your life. You can expect growth to pick up steam soon, there is a goal that arrives to inspire your mind. Gaining traction on your vision does bring a path which dazzles with potential. Friendship takes center stage in your life. You have untapped strengths that are given an avenue for expression. It does see fantastic new potential arriving that helps you launch towards developing your skillset. You can embrace this forward-moving energy, there is the advancement that draws a new endeavor. It brings an enticing path towards areas of learning and crafting your talents.

There is positive news coming, it brings a time of expanding opportunity. You draw luck and good fortune, and this sees you embarking on an adventurous chapter. Broadening your horizons does generate new leads and places you in the box seat to develop a friendship that inspires your mind. Hearty discussions bring trailblazing ideas to mull over.

The New Moon in Leo this week begins a new chapter. There is potential coming, it brings social opportunities, and kicks of refresh cycle of growth for your social life. You have a busy time ahead, news arrives to tempt you into a community environment. It brings a chapter that inspires and motivates you to connect with kindred spirits. Lively communications draw abundance, there is harmony in your surroundings. These talks sprinkle your life with excitement and possibility. Your presence fills with energy and enthusiasm, ensuring you hit the ground running towards a fresh start. You enter an expressive time that sees the areas of self and identity come into focus. It does heighten creativity, you feel energized, and focus on developing a space that brings great joy into your life. A life-changing epiphany may soon see you heading in a new direction. It is a time that is inspiring, you can craft new dreams and develop your vision. Old outworn areas are dissolved, this brings new potential. You can utilize the powers of manifestation to transition to a new chapter. It does see you facing an important decision, contemplating options at the crossroads, help you make a final choice. You follow a path that turns the tables in your favor. It is a process of resolving issues and building foundations that enable you to feel emotionally secure.

Excitement and inspiration figure prominently in the next few days. A situation that has been problematic in the past does improve, and this brings you a sense of abundance. The energy which is brewing is nurturing, versatile, and rewarding. It lets you work on building a stable platform from which to create the next chapter of growth. There are opportunities to improve your circumstances. There is support from the universe to help you expand your horizons into an area that kicks off a constant cycle of growth. Taking advantage of heightened opportunities, you hit upon an area which holds significant potential for progression. It leads to a robust and productive chapter, it is the beginning of something big for you. You are moving towards a new beginning, which holds the promise of substantial benefit. You resonate with a sense of authenticity, which is undeniable, and this really allows you to come into your own unique talents. You incorporate the lessons learned into a new chapter. You turn a corner and upgrade your situation in a big way. Focusing on the essentials brings you towards building the right foundations needed to achieve a connection that brings joy.

This is a great time to release areas that have held you back. You find new ideas soon give you a burst of optimism. You are set to usher in a chapter that is brighter and holds the promise of supporting your goals. You make meaningful headway in crucial areas of your life that have been bringing your energy down. This creates a shift in your emotional outlook, which is positive and a refreshing change.

The Full Moon in Aquarius at the beginning of this week is also a rare blue moon. There are some lovely changes set to flow into your life. A new understanding enters your world, which is restorative to your energy. Harnessing the blissful power of peace, this energy brings you wisdom and insight into your future goals. An area is calling to be developed, and spending time reflecting on your hopes and dreams will provide you with a direction to head towards. News also arrives, which should be considered a signpost. Prioritizing and streamlining enables you to move forward and increase a strong sense of security in your world. You can soon be celebrating a sense of freedom. Opportunities to improve your circumstances abound. This support from the universe is fundamental in seeing you enter an ongoing cycle of growth. With the wind beneath your wings, you are unstoppable and can increase your personal abilities. You are ready to embrace more fun in your life. Celebrations are coming, which enable you to break free of limitations and magically expand your horizons. Your inspiration is shining brightly, you are being guided to look at long-term goals and determine whether they are still in alignment with your core vision. You hone in on a new exciting endeavor; this presents itself as a page-turning opportunity. It increases your motivation, your inspiration, and imagination run wild. Throwing caution to the wind, you begin to make strides towards achieving your most cherished dreams. It is time to broaden your horizons and explore an especially uplifting path. Your fiery optimism searches for the right fit, finding your passion revolutionizes your situation.

September 7 - New Moon in Virgo.

The Moon is on the same side of the Earth as the Sun and will not be visible in the night sky. This phase occurs at 00:52 UTC. This is an excellent time to observe galaxies and stars because there is no moonlight visible.

September 13 – First Quarter Moon in Sagittarius.

This Moon phase occurs at 20.39 UTC.

September 14 - Neptune at Opposition.

The giant blue planet will be at its closest approach to Earth, and its face will be illuminated by the Sun. This event occurs at 08:00 UTC.

September 14 - Mercury at Greatest Eastern Elongation.

The planet Mercury reaches greatest eastern elongation of 23.8 degrees from the Sun. This event occurs at 04:00 UTC. This is the best time to view Mercury. Look for the planet low in the western sky just after sunset.

September 20 - Full Moon in Pisces.

The Moon is on the opposite side of the Earth as the Sun, and its face will be fully illuminated. This phase occurs at 23:55 UTC. Full Corn Moon. This moon is also known as the Harvest Moon. The Harvest Moon is the full moon that occurs closest to the September equinox each year.

September 22 - September Equinox.

The 2021 September equinox occurs at 19:21 UTC. The Sun shines directly on the equator, creating equal amounts of day and night throughout the world. This is also autumnal equinox in the northern hemisphere and is considered a significant zodiac event for many traditional cultures.

September 27 – Mercury Retrograde begins in Libra.

During a retrograde period, it isn't the right time to move forward in any practical venture. Be prepared for misunderstandings and miscommunications to be more prevalent.

September 29 – Last Quarter Moon in Cancer.

This Moon phase occurs at 01.57 UTC.

It is a time that gets you back to basics. There is a lot of activity coming, and this shines a light on developing an enterprising area. It resonates in an ever-widening circle of new options to tempt you forward. It is the ticket for a productive chapter that draws abundance and joy. Welcome news arrives that lights a path forward. It represents something enterprising that gets you thinking big about the potential possible. As you visualize your future goals, you reveal an area that is ready to develop. You shift your focus towards this project, creating growth, and activating creative abilities to stunning effect. It does seem that you're able to reshape potential and revolutionize your environment. It sees some issues being removed soon, this helps create a shift forward, you enter a more prosperous cycle and explore new options which bring great happiness. It is a fruitful time that invites you to expand your horizons. The energy of manifestation has you thinking about your future goals. There is new energy ready to flow into your world, keeping open to change does see you spot the gem amongst the rubble. Discovering an option that inspires fuels your creativity dynamically, it encourages you to dive deep and expand your horizons. Fresh ideas flow into your world, it is a time that brings the exciting potential to the forefront of your life. An echo of the past also influences your outlook. This enables you to reflect on what has gone before, it can bring up sensitive emotions, this is part of the healing process, it improves the stability possible in your world by enabling you time to process difficult emotions, and resolve outworn energy. It is a time that helps you cut away from the deadwood and embrace a new flow of potential soon.

Neptune at opposition occurs at the end of this week. Neptune rules your house of dreams and healing. There have been some issues that have not been helping your situation, digging deeper and getting to the heart of the matter does help you remove the deadwood. Additionally, your willingness to open yourself to new experiences and people is instrumental in drawing better options into your world. Fundamental changes are coming, this rewards you with opportunities for growth and expression. You begin to get a sense that things are shifting forward, and this reveals that your conditions are changing; there is a desire to expand your life and draw abundance. In fact, options are coming into your world that supports a journey of change. Growth picks up an active pace, it does bring a buzz of excitement that has you more confident about stepping out into a new area.

Furthermore, this week brings a more social environment, and having some good company is a beautiful balm for your spirit. It is a particular time for you; it does see more social opportunities arrive, which nurtures your soul. It is the perfect recipe for renewal, rejuvenation, and kicking back with your kindred spirits. An invitation to an event arrives, and this is extra special, you mark this in your calendar, and look forward to an exciting and vibrant time. There is plenty to be inspired about over the coming chapter, it is a time of abundance.

You discover it is smooth sailing, and as you steer your ship into uncharted waters, you can release any pressure or anxiety that binds your spirit up into tight knots. Give yourself leeway to explore and harness that sense of the pioneering inspiration that takes you further. It does seem that this is going to be a highly creative time, listening to your inner voice guides you towards areas that offer room to grow your talents. A positive influence shines a light on a warm and abundant future. It is a time that charms and delights, you weave beautiful moments into a chapter that is brimming with exciting potential. It does offer a path that you treasure, and if you've had difficulties in the past, you discover an open road of potential glimmers ahead. You reap many rewards through your willingness to move forward towards a brighter chapter. An opportunity arriving, which puts the spotlight on your leadership abilities. You can look forward to impressive results that increase stability, ambition, and advancement. Decisions are best made with a calm mind, and with a strategic mindset. It brings a busy and productive time that improves your bottom line. You land in an area that offers room to grow your abilities as you manifest results that bring heightened security. You touch down on some enticing new options soon, this has you reaching for your dreams. It does see positive change arriving to tempt you towards pushing back boundaries and stepping out of your comfort zone. It is helping you achieve an impressive outcome, having a fixed goal in your mind, does see you taking the steps necessary to climb the ladder of success. A sunny aspect arrives to light a path forward

The Equinox this week speaks of a golden opportunity arriving to inspire your mind and shift your focus forward. It does bring quite an exciting time, a variety of options make themselves known, and this is terrific news. It is a happy chapter packed full of goodness to lift your spirits higher. Natural forces work in your favor to help develop a personal dream. Information reaches you shortly, that creates a breakthrough moment. It does see a situation turning in your favor. Knowing the truth does bring clarity. You discover someone is willing to step up and prove worth, it brings a time that draws a closer bond to light. Focusing your energy on this situation accomplishes a positive outcome. It is a time that brings unexpected news; this sees progress occurring soon afterward. A time of expansion brings a bountiful chapter. While you outgrow certain friendships, it does bring a shift forward, which entices you to explore a new social environment. Staying open to new options does have a ripple effect, it brings you beyond what you previously thought was possible. It rebuilds your social life, and a new friendship soon blossoms. You get busy crafting your dreams into something tangible. You leave a strong impression on another person. It does see a bond blossoming; it brings a fascinating chapter that encourages you to take a leap of faith. It does connect you to a sociable time, goals you set in motion gently unfold. Your life feels blessed with excitement, it does bring a vital shift forward. Sharing thoughts with the emotionally intelligent one is a breath of fresh air. It brings a sense of rejuvenation, it connects you with a time that highlights happiness and joy.

October 6 - New Moon in Libra.

The New Moon speaks of something new arriving in your world. This moon phase occurs at 11:05 UTC. This is an excellent time of the month to view galaxies and stars because there is no moonlight visible.

October 7 - Draconids Meteor Shower.

The Draconids meteor shower runs annually from October 6-10 and peaks this year on the night of the 7th.

October 8 – Mars in Conjunction with the Sun.

The planet Mars in Conjunction with the Sun. This occurs at 04:00 UTC.

October 9 – Mercury at Inferior Conjunction.

The planet Mercury at Inferior Conjunction. This planetary event occurs at 16:00 UTC.

October 13 – First Quarter Moon in Capricorn.

This Moon phase occurs at 03.25 UTC.

October 18 – Mercury Retrograde ends in Libra.

You can now move forward with any delayed plans that you have been putting off due to the Mercury Retrograde phase. Relationships should soon improve as miscommunications are overcome

October 20 - Full Moon in Aries.

The October full Moon is on the opposite side of the Earth as the Sun and will be fully illuminated. This phase occurs at 14:57 UTC. This full moon is known as the Hunters Moon. Powerful energy lights a path forward. You can attract and manifest excellent results during the complete moon phase.

October 21, 22 - Orionids Meteor Shower.

The Orionids meteor shower runs yearly from October 2 to November 7. Orionids meteor shower peaks this year on the night of October 21 and the morning of October 22.

October 25 - Mercury at Greatest Western Elongation.

The planet Mercury reaches greatest western elongation of 18.4 degrees from the Sun. Look for Mercury low in the eastern sky just before sunrise. This event occurs at 05:00 UTC.

October 28 – Last Quarter Moon in Leo.

This Moon phase occurs at 20.05 UTC.

October 29 - Venus Greatest Eastern Elongation.

The planet Venus reaches its greatest eastern elongation of 47 degrees from the Sun. This is the best time to view Venus. Look for the bright planet Venus in the western sky after sunset. This planetary phase occurs at 22.00 UTC.

You get closer to a goal soon, it does see you working in tandem with another. It is an exciting time that draws change. Taking full advantage of the potential which emerges does place a big focus on advancing your situation. An invitation arrives that gives you a hint of the activity which is ready to flow into your world. Gorgeous conversations bring lively discussions. This brings new and exciting people into your life, it does see friendships becoming a focal point, exploring the possibilities ramps up the potential in your social life. They have much to contribute, lively conversations draw abundance, and new ideas put a spring in your step. There is a remarkable growth to be achieved by developing these new acquaintances and friendships. You are ready to dive into a new chapter, it does bring an enchanting phase of expanding your social circle. There is a great deal of activity coming which makes this a particular time, you become more involved in community endeavors, this is a breath of fresh air that sees new bonds being formed. You catch up with friends, and this begins to take on a more significant role in your life. Opportunities arrive that see you grow. In fact, your talents continue to increase, your star is ready to burn brightly. It may seem that life comes full circle and gives you a second chance to achieve a dream that has been on the back burner for some time. Taking advantage of opportunities that come your way brings you to a new chapter. You discover a path of passion, creativity, and self-expression. There is a change that resonates brightly in your world. It brings a sense of healing and a breakthrough that offers you room to spread your wings.

Mars, in conjunction with the Sun this week, lets you pop the cork on the genie's bottle. It brings a sudden and dramatic entrance that requires your attention. Reevaluating the situation at hand, you can remove areas that are not helpful, and by getting rid of the deadwood, you break down your issues, and begin the process of rebuilding your life to create more stable foundations. Mars is an attention grabber, you discover there is something that requires decisive action. It is an excellent time for removing areas that limit progress. Once you have dealt with the problem that you face, you can begin the process of rebuilding your life following the wisdom you have garnered through your ability to overcome hurdles and come out on top. Tenacity and determination see you rise above any issues that you face over the coming days. You are determined to improve your situation, news arrives that sees an offer appearing. It does have you thinking about the possibilities, there may be some adjustments required to entirely focus on revealing this option. Taking full advantage of this journey brings the right environment for growth. You begin to see changes that are the result of your hard work and dedication. An exciting possibility makes itself known, this is one you should take full advantage of developing. It does bring a new adventure, and this touches off a chapter that brings excitement and fun to life. There is more activity arriving that brings new friendships. It does give a hint of how special your social life is going to be this year. Life is busy, it positions you to stay open to invitations and opportunities.

This is a time that grows your world. Constraints are lifted when Mercury Retrograde ends this week; your situation expands outwardly. You are ready to drive forward towards achieving some crucial goals. Setting your sights on your vision does align your path correctly. Brainstorming ideas with another helps you come up with a strategy that brings results. You have the positive energy of manifestation surrounding your situation, it does give you a strong indication that things are ready to shift forward. A chapter is coming, which is in alignment with your core vision. A key area emerges which brings new potential. You discover an enterprise that is ripe for development, it does see your diligence and attention to detail is rewarded with a situation that advances quickly. Movement and discovery are at the basis of this appealing chapter. It is a time of good luck and inspiring goals.

This Full Moon in Aries is about healing the past, including any blockages, does bring a new chapter potential into your life. It takes you to a lighter time and connects you with others that draw healing. You open a gateway towards a new time of life. There is a necessary transition occurring, part of this process is letting go, and moving away from a situation which has caused you sadness. You are ready to resolve complicated emotions and release any areas that hold you back. You are given a chance to dive into a new chapter soon, a window of opportunity is opening, and something individual breezes into your world to inspire your mind and shift your focus towards developing an exciting vision. A new friendship is in the stars for you soon.

An opportunity arriving that provides you with a valuable outlet. It does bring rejuvenation, a superb option sparks forward motion activity, it does connect you with others, a more social vibe creates room to embrace new friendships. It is a busy and active time, drawing a prosperous cycle to light. This is an ideal time to create space for new potential in your world. You are ready to break free of constraints and dive into a new chapter of potential. Your willingness to explore new avenues does spark a time of expansion and growth. A whole modern philosophy may soon arise from your desire to learn new areas. A life-changing moment sweeps into your life, it brings inspiration and heralds the start of something special. A revelation brings enlightenment, it leads to a breakthrough in your personal life. You discover a bond is possible with one who touches your heart, it does bring a journey that sees you taking a leap of faith and embracing a time of excitement and expansion. It is a potent chapter that takes you towards essential life changes. You discover a situation that is worthy of your devotion. Progression soon follows. A myriad of opportunities ready to flow into your life. It helps you to take advantage of a time that offers room to grow your vision. Focusing on your goals becomes a priority, it brings options that enable you to build your talents. Your innate skills and abilities hold you in good stead, it reveals a path that brings joy. It does seem that you can trust your instincts on this one. Your prospects are about to become rosier, it does lift the lid on a chapter of potential that enables you to chase your dreams and expand your world.

November 4 - New Moon in Scorpio.

The New Moon brings a clean chapter of potential. This phase occurs at 21:15 UTC. This is an excellent time to view the stars because there is no moonlight visible.

November 5 - Uranus at Opposition.

The blue-green planet will be at its closest approach to Earth, and its face will be fully illuminated by the Sun. This event occurs at 00:00 UTC.

November 11 – First Quarter Moon in Aquarius.

This Moon phase occurs at 12.46 UTC.

November 12 - Taurids Meteor Shower.

The Taurids meteor shower runs yearly from September 7 to December 10. It peaks on the night of November 12.

November 17 - Partial Lunar Eclipse

A partial lunar eclipse occurs when the Moon passes through the Earth's partial shadow or penumbra, only a portion of it passes through the umbra. During this eclipse, part of the Moon darkens as it moves through the Earth's shadow. This partial lunar eclipse will be visible throughout most of eastern Russia, Japan, the Pacific Ocean, North America, Mexico, Central America, and parts of western South America.

November 17, 18 - Leonids Meteor Shower.

The Leonids meteor shower runs yearly from November 6-30. The Leonids meteor shower peaks this year on the night of the 17th and morning of the 18th.

November 19 - Full Moon in Taurus.

The Full Moon is on the opposite side of the Earth as the Sun and will appear fully illuminated. This phase occurs at 08:58 UTC. This full moon is known as Full Beaver Moon. Powerful energy lights a path forward. You can attract and manifest excellent results during the complete moon phase.

November 27 – Last Quarter Moon in Virgo.

This Moon phase occurs at 12.28 UTC.

November 29 – Mercury at Superior Conjunction.

The planet Mercury at Superior Conjunction. This planetary event occurs at 05:00 UTC.

The New Moon in Scorpio this week brings insight, clarity, and awareness. Life holds a bounty of refreshing options, there is abundance on offer, broadening your perception does bring a new endeavor to light. It's the perfect way to reinvent your trajectory, being adaptable to change lets you make the most of the enterprising a chapter ahead. A high-level option arrives that sees progress occurring around a long term goal. You can create the change you have been seeking. Standing at the crossroads, you utilize the wisdom of the past and step into where the future tempts you forward. You are headed towards a phase of transformation, a new avenue of growth emerges, it brings essential changes that leave you feeling energized. You can forge a path towards obtaining your vision. It does bring surprise news into your life soon. Opportunities to mingle and network are arriving soon. Your confidence is on the rise, this brings people into your circle, it does offer a new friendship that inspires your mind. You can expect a big reveal soon, this information arrives to tempt you forward. It brings an extraordinary chapter where things fall into place, it does have you contemplating exciting new potential with an open heart. You are transitioning to a new phase that is going to be much easier; you're finishing up a cycle that has been draining and demanding. It's all led towards growing your spirit, your pioneering personality is ready to seek a new adventure. A new option gives you an open road to explore, it does connect you with a diverse background, someone you meet becomes an important focus.

The Taurids meteor shower, which peaks on November 12th this year, see your potential shine brightly. You may be stuck in a rut and moving towards new experiences is going to benefit your situation. It does bring remarkable options that grow your world, and this is a rejuvenating boost to your spirit. It brings a happy time filled with new possibilities that lift your spirits. It marks the beginning of an exciting chapter that is blessed with surprises. An exciting prospect that makes itself known soon. You will be in the box seat to take advantage of an exciting episode. It brings new options that feed your inspiration, you launch your talents on a path that brings favorable outcomes. It does see a conversation ahead that gets you thinking about the possibilities. You have a beautiful ability to bring sunshine into the world. Your ideas and creativity come together with a flourish, and this sees an endeavor opening that may be a good fit for your artistic abilities. You have a great deal to give back to your wider community. An option arrives that is the perfect fit, and this brings a flurry of activity. Releasing the doubt does draw confidence, you become involved in a passion project that brings sunshine into your life. It does offer room to expand your social life. A team project may even crop up that fits your vision perfectly.

A Partial Lunar Eclipse on the 17th brings a landmark moment, it is a gateway toward a brighter future. This Lunar Eclipse speaks about a second chance, arriving soon for you. It does seem that you are on the right path to advance a personal goal. Something lands in your lap that bring you a thrilling surprise, it is a situation you are keen to pursue. Listening to your intuition does guide you towards a chapter of happiness and harmony. Life becomes productive and joyful. If things are not currently ideal, this cosmic event is the currency of change. Circulating in your wider community does bring new options that let you move forward. Good luck and fortune are ready to flow into your world. You may soon receive notice of an exciting, unique opportunity that gets the ball rolling on an enterprising chapter. You can consider this as the beginning of a transformation. You are ready to embrace a more social chapter. Your situation is currently evolving, something arrives that requires your immediate attention, noticing this option does bring you to a productive section that draws new friendships to light. Things turn out well; it brings an exciting moment and lines you up beautifully toward a more expansive environment. You can take advantage of a rosy trend by exploring options that inspire your mind. It does see new and existing friends arriving, you explore possibilities that help you evolve. It does bring good cheer and social interactions. Getting involved with your wider community does bring the most exceptional personal growth. Things are on the move for you in a manner that you currently may not realize. It does bring a shift forward that transitions you toward a chapter that offers room to grow your life.

This week speaks of change arriving soon. It does help to heal old areas that have clung to your spirit recently. Someone of importance makes a debut in your life soon, it does see you shift your focus forward and build foundations that offer room to grow your situation. It's time to nurture your growth and plant the seeds that grow into something spectacular. This is a turning point that brings new options to your table, this speaks about the news arriving soon that is curious, it sparks your interest offers you the chance to explore a new lead. This potential takes you toward a journey of change, you soon get a clearer picture, it is a time that brings excitement and activity into your life. You turn a corner and headed towards growth, your willingness to persevere does draw dividends. A goal you've had for a while soon comes into focus. It does bring a burst of energy that enables you to make substantial progress on your vision. Things come together, it no longer feels up in the air. You enter an enchanting chapter of developing your life on your terms. It does draw abundance, you have the Golden touch, and can step boldly forward into a new chapter. Life begins to flow more easily, it brings exciting options to contemplate. It is an excellent time to organize, prioritize, and streamline your environment as life is about to get busy. You diverge from your usual path and head off on an adventure that calls your spirit. It does reveal a creative journey that develops your talents. It may even lead to a new trajectory that inspires your mind. A social situation emerges that is a salve that transitions you to a happy time.

DECEMBER ASTROLOGY

December 4 - New Moon in Sagittarius.

The New Moon brings a clean slate of potential. This moon phase occurs at 07:43 UTC. This is an excellent time to view galaxies and stars because there is no moonlight visible.

December 4 – Total Solar Eclipse.

A total solar eclipse occurs when the moon completely blocks the Sun, revealing the Sun's outer atmosphere, which is called the corona. The path of totality will, for this eclipse, be limited to Antarctica and the southern Atlantic Ocean. A partial eclipse will bee visible throughout much of South Africa.

December 11 – First Quarter Moon in Pisces.

This Moon phase occurs at 01.36 UTC.

December 13, 14,15 - Geminids Meteor Shower.

The Geminids meteor shower runs each year from December 7-17. The Geminids meteor showers peaks this year on the night of the 13th, 14th, and 15th. The nearly new moon this year will provide dark skies for an excellent show. Best viewing will be from a dim vista after midnight. Meteors will radiate from the constellation Gemini but can appear anywhere in the sky.

December 19 - Full Moon in Gemini.

The Full Moon illuminates and draws clarity. This moon phase occurs at 04:36 UTC. This full moon is known as the Cold Moon and the Moon Before Yule. Powerful energy lights a path forward. You can attract and manifest excellent results during the full moon phase.

December 21 - December Solstice.

The 2021 December solstice occurs at 15:59 UTC. The South Pole of the earth tilts toward the Sun, which, having reached its most southern place in the sky, is directly over the Tropic of Capricorn at 23.44 degrees south latitude. This December solstice also marks the first day of winter in the Northern Hemisphere.

December 21, 22 - Ursids Meteor Shower.

The Ursids meteor shower occurs each year from December 17 - 25. This meteor event peaks this year on the night of the 21st and morning of the 22nd.

December 27 – Last Quarter Moon in Libra.

This Moon phase occurs at 02.24 UTC.

December hits the right kind of positive note that you need in your life. An offer arrives, and it does have you thinking about the potential possible, you shift your focus forwards, a newfound sense of freedom draws adventure into your life. This is a time that brings gifts and luck into your life. It syncs you up with a chapter that offers a new role, you negotiate a path that grows your talents. It's important to note that you can expand your life and learn about these new areas. You are capable of much more than you are currently involved with. Something is coming up that creates a buzz of excitement in your world. A new option arrives, which is a jewel, this gem is perfect for your life. It does give you a chance to proceed forward, it brings new pathways of growth and abundance. This favorable option arrives by surprise; it comes out of the blue but leaves you feeling excited about the potential possible. It is an ideal time to grow your life and explore new options. This is a time that sees a lovely setting that lands you in an environment that brings enrichment into your world. A sense of rejuvenation is so refreshing, it brings new options and does spark and adventurous aspect that has you open to new experiences. It is a necessary time that sparks personal growth, by looking at the possibilities surrounding you, you may spot the jewel in your crown. It does bring new experiences that leave you feeling inspired. Your restless spirit is guiding you to step out of your comfort zone and mark a bold path toward your future. It does position you well to learn a new area.

This is a time that offers you room to grow your goals. Focusing on improving your situation does raise you above uncertainty, it takes you on a path that provides stability, security, and advancement. Your job is evolving, there are opportunities ahead to pursue a route that speaks volumes to the person you are becoming. There is a focus on creativity and on self-development. You have faced the difficulties of the past with courage, you now are ready to draw healing and rejuvenation. It does see a fresh flow of energy arriving that kicks off a new chapter for you. It is a fruitful time to explore your options as you face the future; there is an open road of potential before you. It does see a time that draws abundance and joy arriving soon. You reach a crossroads, and at this intersection, you are faced with two choices. Using the wisdom you have gathered, you discern the correct avenue to explore. It does shut the door on a chapter that has drained your energy, you are ready to explore new options and process any heavy emotions that hold you back. Taking a leap of faith rewards you with an exciting time of personal growth. Your positive outlook is going to come in handy, you are ready to make strides on developing your goals and setting positive intentions does let you focus on the essential steps necessary to achieve your vision. As you flex your creativity, you are rewarded with an option you can bank on. It does create a shift that shakes up your environment and brings you an avenue to develop further.

News is coming within weeks, it does let you plot a course towards an exciting enterprise. It carries you forward towards building new foundations. As you secure your plan for the future, you discover that things are not as challenging to progress as first feared. You soon gain traction on your vision, drawing abundance into your world. An exciting chapter is arriving soon. It does see your potential bloom, a random conversation sparks a new interest. This venture has a long reach, taking an active role in developing the potential does bring a unique friendship to light. Lively discussions and the sharing of thoughts and ideas creates a landscape of abundance. It is worthwhile exploring new avenues of growth. There is a fulfillment of a goal arriving in your life, this releases limitations, your progress is no longer held back, as you reach a turning point, you're able to reshape your potential, and revolutionize your environment. This is a journey of abundance, stability and security. You attend an event and attract the attention of an admirer. Your personal magnetism is on the rise, this is drawing you closer to a situation which offers an intriguing sense of chemistry. It is a time where you are expressly focused on developing a personal area. This is a time which draws options that delight, it is a memorable and tender chapter, there is much on offer, it is the perfect time to expand your life and look at areas which draw abundance. There is good news coming, this leads to some excitement in your house. You may be making some individual plans before long, and enjoy a bustle of new activity.

You are set to enter an optimistic chapter, it offers you options to circulate, this social growth does inspire a light-hearted environment. It has you spending time with friends and family. This lights your life with rejuvenating and refreshing energy. It is an ideal time to visualize your dreams and heal areas that have limited progress in your life. You enter a grounded chapter soon, which brings the balance back into your life. Restoring and renewing your soul brings you back in sync with other opportunities that surround your world. It does plant your goals in solid ground, it offers you a chance to expand your horizons, which culminates in an exciting offer crossing your path soon, things to come together with a flourish. It's time to review the past, taking inventory helps you decide future goals. Moving in alignment with your vision does see you investing your time correctly. It enables you to discard areas that do not resonate with your higher purpose. There are adventures close by; this draws a bustling phase of activity into being; it offers enterprising options that speak to your innovative mind. Creating space to pause and reflect does attract peace into your life. It sees the future shimmering with new potential, you emerge from your sanctuary feeling renewed and ready to take on the world. Your prospects are rising, this brings new options to explore. Troublesome energy is released; this allows you to focus on making progress. Something arrives, out of the blue, it feels like pure chance, but is perfect for your situation. You begin to see a broader picture of what is possible when you make yourself a priority, fortune favors the bold, this sees your potential blossoming, it shines a light on a path which is refreshing and exciting.

Dear Stargazer,

I hope you have enjoyed planning your year with the stars utilizing Astrology and Zodiac influences. My zodiac star sign books are released each year, which detail a monthly list of astrological events, and a unique weekly (four weeks to a month) horoscope. You can find me on my Facebook page where you can get personal astrology or intuitive readings.

https://www.facebook.com/SiaSands

Instagram: SiaSands

See my full list of books here:

https://www.SiaSands.com

Leaving a review is welcomed and appreciated.

Many Blessings,

Sia Sands

www.ingramcontent.com/pod-product-compliance
Lightning Source LLC
Chambersburg PA
CBHW031141250726
48655CB00002B/779